Swimming

Like a Pro

Aaron Carr

www.av2books.com

Step 1
Go to **www.av2books.com**

Step 2
Enter this unique code

XZIPW0KZM

Step 3
Explore your interactive eBook!

AV2

Like a Pro

Swimming

Start!

AV2 is optimized for use on any device

Your interactive eBook comes with...

Read

Audio
Listen to the entire book read aloud

Videos
Watch informative video clips

Weblinks
Gain additional information for research

Try This!
Complete activities and hands-on experiments

Key Words
Study vocabulary, and complete a matching word activity

Quizzes
Test your knowledge

Slideshows
View images and captions

View new titles and product videos at
www.av2books.com

Swimming

Contents

I love swimming.
I am going swimming today.

4

Like a Pro

Swimming was
part of the
first modern
Olympic Games.

I get ready to go swimming. I bring my swimsuit.

Swimsuits can help people swim faster.

I also wear a swim cap when I swim. It helps keep water out of my hair.

Swim caps help swimmers move through water.

I go to the pool to swim. I put my swimsuit on in the dressing room.

Swimming pools are often split into lanes.

11

I stretch before getting into the pool. I also do some warm up laps in the pool.

Like a Pro

Warming up helps the body get ready to swim.

13

I swim in a race with other swimmers. The fastest swimmer wins the race.

Swimmers begin races from starting blocks.

I race in different events. Each event uses a different kind of swimming stroke.

There are four
main strokes
in swimming.

I am part of a swim team.
We all wear the same
swimsuit and cap colors.

18

Like a Pro

Swim teams race together in relay events.

I love swimming.

SWIMMING FACTS

This page provides more detail about the interesting facts found in the book. Simply look at the corresponding page number to match the fact.

Pages 4–5

What Is Swimming? People have taken part in swimming competitions for thousands of years. Early swimming races were held in natural bodies of water, such as lakes and rivers. The ancient Romans were the first to build swimming pools. However, competitive swimming did not become widespread until the 19th century, when the first swimming organizations formed. In 1896, the first modern Olympic Games featured four swimming events.

Pages 6–7

What I Wear Swimsuits can be as simple as a pair of swimming shorts for boys or a one- or two-piece swimsuit for girls. These swimsuits are worn for comfort or appearance. Competition swimsuits help people swim faster. Girls wear one-piece suits that cover them from the shoulders to the hips. Other types also cover the arms and upper legs to the knees. Boys can wear swimming briefs or jammers. Briefs leave all of the leg bare, while jammers extend to just above the knees.

Pages 8–9

What I Need In addition to the swimsuit, most swimmers also wear a swim cap. A swim cap is a tight cap made from a rubber-like material, such as silicone or latex. The swim cap covers a swimmer's hair and the tops of the ears. This helps swimmers cut through the water more easily and swim faster. It also helps them keep water out of their ears and chlorine out of their hair. Some swimmers also like to wear goggles to keep water out of their eyes.

Pages 10–11

Where I Swim People can swim in almost any body of water, as long as it is large and deep enough for swimming. However, competitive swimming is most often done in indoor swimming pools. Most swimming competitions are held in Olympic pools. These pools are 160 feet (50 meters) long, 82 feet (25 m) wide, and at least 6.6 feet (2 m) deep. The pool is divided into eight lanes that are separated by colored ropes.

Warming Up It is a good idea to warm up before swimming in a race. A good warm-up routine may include a variety of stretches and some light practice laps in the swimming pool. Stretching loosens muscles and helps prevent injury, while practice laps get the body ready to perform. It is best to start a warm-up routine with slow, careful movements and build up to more intense exercise near the end of the warm-up.

Starting a Race Races begin with swimmers lined up behind raised platforms, or starting blocks, at one end of the pool. When a long whistle sounds, the swimmers step onto the starting blocks. The starter then tells the swimmers to take their marks. The swimmers get into position. A start signal, either from a starter pistol or an electronic starting device, marks the beginning of the race. The swimmers dive into the pool and begin swimming.

Different Strokes There are four swimming strokes used in competitions. These are freestyle, breaststroke, backstroke, and butterfly. Swimmers can enter races in all four strokes. There are also several different events for each stroke, usually ranging from 25 m to 1,500 m. In medley events, swimmers use all four strokes in one race. In recent years, many swimmers have begun using another technique, called a dolphin kick, when changing direction at the end of the pool.

Part of the Team Most swimmers compete as part of a swim team. Teams earn points based on how well their members perform in each event. The top six swimmers in each event earn points for their teams, with first-place scoring the most points. The team with the most points wins the team competition. There is also a team medley event. In this race, four teammates take turns swimming, with each person performing a different stroke in his or her section, or leg, of the race.

I Love Swimming Swimming is a great way to stay active and healthy. It is a fast-paced, high-energy sport that requires strength, stamina, and skill. Swimming promotes physical fitness and cardiovascular health. However, swimming alone is not enough to stay healthy. In order to get the most benefit from swimming, it is also important to eat healthful foods. Foods such as fruits, vegetables, and grains give the body the energy it needs to perform its best.

KEY WORDS

Research has shown that as much as 65 percent of all written material published in English is made up of 300 words. These 300 words cannot be taught using pictures or learned by sounding them out. They must be recognized by sight. This book contains 48 common sight words to help young readers improve their reading fluency and comprehension. This book also teaches young readers several important content words, such as proper nouns. These words are paired with pictures to aid in learning and improve understanding.

Page	Sight Words First Appearance	Page	Content Words First Appearance
4	am, I	4	swimming
5	a, first, like, of, part, the, was	5	Olympic Games, pro
6	get, go, my, to	6	swimsuit
7	can, help, people	8	hair, swim cap
8	also, it, keep, out, water, when	9	swimmers
9	move, through	10	dressing room, pool
10	in, on, put	11	lanes
11	are, into, often	12	laps
12	before, do, some, up	13	body
14	other, with	14	race
15	from	15	starting blocks
16	different, each, kind, uses	16	events, swimming stroke
17	four, there	18	colors, swim team
18	all, and, same, we	19	relay events
19	together		

Published by AV2
350 5th Avenue, 59th Floor, New York, NY 10118
Website: www.av2books.com

042020
100919

Printed in Guangzhou, China
1 2 3 4 5 6 7 8 9 0 24 23 22 21 20

Project Coordinator: John Willis
Designer: Ana María Vidal

Library of Congress Control Number: 2020935056

ISBN 978-1-7911-2736-7 (hardcover)
ISBN 978-1-7911-2761-9 (softcover)
ISBN 978-1-7911-2762-6 (multi-user eBook)
ISBN 978-1-7911-2763-3 (single-user eBook)

Every reasonable effort has been made to trace ownership and to obtain permission to reprint copyright material. The publisher would be pleased to have any errors or omissions brought to its attention so that they may be corrected in subsequent printings.

The publisher acknowledges Alamy, Getty Images, iStock, and Shutterstock as its primary image suppliers for this title.